mindoßerenity

mindofserenity

mindofserenity

JOURNEY OF A TAINTED HEART

―――――――――――――――――――

© *2022 mindofserenity*

All Rights Reserved

mindoserenity

mindoßerenity

To my most beloved and the love that is ever given to me.
To those who had stayed and listened. To those that had shown me kindness in this journey. To those that had welcomed me and shared the beauty of Islam with me.

I cannot have pursued this dream of mine. We have come a long way and I am grateful for the meeting of many beautiful souls.
I am uttermost grateful to Allah subḥānahu wataʿālā that made this all possible.

Without Him, I would not be here today.
لِلَّهِ ٱلْحَمْدُ

mindofserenity

CONTENTS

Chapter 1

The Escape   15

Chapter 2

The Encounter   43

Chapter 3

The Finding   73

Chapter 4

The Lessons   99

Chapter 5

The Promise   141

Poetry

The Beginning   167

AUTHOR'S NOTE

In all that I have done, all that I have said, all that I have written and hadn't, there is one that I knew that is promising;
Allah knows while the world does not.
Truly, that for me is enough.

I cannot deny what has stayed with me growing up as a catholic, which to this day has provided the basis of my values and morals. Only through becoming Muslim has elevated them.
On January 25th, 2020, the day I reverted had only enhanced and beautified the qualities that I have now learned to cherish. The day I reverted has transformed every struggle I have carried to be a wisdom-filled experience. Every lesson I have yet to learn and unlearn, in Allah's given time, will come. I have written this book as a foundation of the lessons I have learned, the journey of how it all began, and the promises to come in the given future. For those who have darkened their hearts, for those searching for the path, for those searching for hope, for those who have lost their light. I pray for those who had laid their eyes in this book will have their hearts laid on to its creator.

As humans, we are naturally interdependent. So if your hearts begin to run for something, as I tend to say, *let it run*. It will always come back and it will not come back alone. The peace we search for in this life can never truly be of a person or a place but is much more divine. In ways, we cannot begin to fathom. Know that the very little part of this peace will always be in the heart before anything else. For some, it takes a lifetime of searching to finally realize where it has been all this time. If the search happens to start from this book, I pray for every step you take on this journey will be a step closer to the righteous, pure truth *insha'Allah* (God-willing).

This is the journey of my tainted heart.

mindofserenity

اللَّهُمَّ إِنِّى أَسْأَلُكَ الْهُدَى وَالتُّقَى وَالْعَفَافَ وَالْغِنَى

Oh Allah! I ask you (to bestow me with) guidance,
God consciousness purity and independence.

رَبَّنَا إِنَّكَ جَامِعُ النَّاسِ لِيَوْمٍ لَا رَيْبَ فِيهِ إِنَّ اللَّهَ لَا يُخْلِفُ الْمِيعَادَ

Our Lord, surely You will gather the people for a Day about which there is no doubt.
Indeed, Allah does not fail in His promise.

Sahih Muslim 2721 | Surah Al-Imran 3:9

mindofserenity

But a pure heart can never be tainted

mindofserenity

A collection of short pieces
for those who escaped,

and found themselves in the wandering.

mindofserenity

THE ESCAPE

Chapter One

The Escape

There will come a time when you feel like a floating boat in the midst of a vast sea. For a single moment, there is tranquility, bliss, and beauty. You become the centre of where the light beams bright. You are happy.

There will also come a time when it feels as though you are the centre of a storm. Slowly, your boat is breaking and breaking until it finally breaks apart. You were once floating. Now you are sinking and shattering. Until all that is left is your broken heart lost at sea.

My very first lesson as I started my journey to finding myself, finding Islam, and finding *Allah* began at a time of my *escape*. My escape from life and what was been tearing me apart. I entered a state of solitude, with a darkened heart and a lifeless mind. There is no good in solitude if there is nothing to long for. For what I wanted for myself, for what I had prayed for, was lost amidst my exile. You may believe that escaping is the answer, that it will lead you to a better life. But in all sincerity from my heart to yours, to escape means leaving behind your blessings. My reversion story began when I believed there was nothing else for me in this life. I was with the wrong people in the wrong places and it was too late for me to go back. In time, little by little, I stopped my daily practices; my prayers, my search for knowledge, and my remembrance. Though I was not Muslim then, I had always believed in something greater, a divine being. I was just not certain. Being a Christian all my life, I was naturally inclined to follow the way of the crowd despite my doubts. I may have once prayed the way they do but my heart was never settled. Though I never pursued this odd curiosity, my routine and lifestyle remained the same. I continued going to church, fulfilling the Christian duties and way of upbringing. I remember my trip to the south of France, Lourdes for a pilgrimage and in search of spiritual healing, though my younger self, of course, did not know best. I later found myself with a new group of people but I was oblivious and naïve enough to oversee the negative impacts it had on me. Slowly, my mentality drastically changed. I was becoming very selfish, arrogant, unkind, and vain.

Before the escape, I faced the reality of a misguided person filled with arrogance and ignorance. I began losing my most sentimental friendships and relationships with my family, purely as a consequence of my pride. I remember envisioning my future life of independence and what I thought to be "freedom"; to live a life without my loved ones. It was all selfish thinking. To believe I would never need them, to never return my gratitude after all the love they had unconditionally given. After I reverted and learned some of the key values of Islam, this would have been a major sin; to cut ties with our kinship. If Allah has forbidden a Muslim to desert his brother for more than 3 days, I cannot imagine how this would be for a lifetime.

As it is hard for me to remember and write this, as the memories come flooding back in that period of my life, I am utmost and utterly grateful for the mercy of Allah *subḥānahu wataʿālā* to change the state of my heart and who I am now as a human being. Though I still have my faults and my weaknesses, I am grateful to have learned from them. To be caught up with life, we tend to look away from what is in front of us. But what we are looking for had always been right under our noses. I was lost. I was searching for my true self but escaping merely leads to losing myself.

Thus, this was my very first mistake, and in a way, this lead to one of my greatest blessings. We have to endure our consequences before we can learn from our lessons.

Abu Huraira reported: The Prophet, peace, and blessings be upon him, said,
"Acknowledge Allah in prosperity and He will acknowledge you in adversity."
Amālī Ibn Bishrān 1365

mindofserenity

The silence of sin has severed the heart in
more ways than fire ever could.

mindofserenity

Go forth,
continue to lift up your hearts to Allah.

To truly know your heart's desires,
let go of your inner voice
and surrender to the path that was created for you.

This *dunya* is simply a door to *Akhirah*.
Where escape is impossible,
without knowing the key.

As things in war are swift and sudden,
so is the knowing of one's heart.
Sooner or later,

everything will all make sense.

mindofserenity

At some point of this journey,
you will realize that no one can give you inner freedom
but Allah.

So be free as the wind,
because for what is written is already yours

and will always be with you.

What *Allah* has written for you
will happen.
Even if everything else tells you the opposite.

People often confuse the works of Allah and the
nature of this world.
Only one of which works in your favour,

that is Allah.

As this world can be cruel but the creator of it is
not cruel to you. For those that rely on *Him*,
is provided and protected.

The soul needs time, for one to learn purity.

To undo who they were.
To be who they need to be.

Maybe this journey is not about learning who we
are supposed to be.
But to unravel the purity of our being.
Becoming what our heart once was.

We are not finding who we are, we are *becoming it.*

We tend to search for light, anywhere we can find it.

Only to forget,
We must also look *inside*.

mindofserenity

Learn the power if your own words,
when it would reach mountains without raising
your voice.

The most beautiful of speech
is beyond our two lips.
To carve one's words,
to inspire, and provoke.
To ignite the flame in our souls.

Listen to how our heart speaks,
its words are beyond mountain peaks.

The magnitude of our love is also very much owed to ourselves.
We *deserve* to be healed as much
as we heal others.

The true eloquence within
is the perseverance you endure.
A resistance against your *nafs*,
the conquer of your inner and worldly desires.

mind☉serenity

To live a life of depth and meaning
comes with afflictions of the heart.
It is a duty for us all,
to purify what plagues it.

mindofserenity

One day it is going to dawn on us.
That this worldly life cannot save us.

My mind wanted the false paradise.

The pleasures of this world,
to seek all that temporary happiness.
The fleeting beauty of this *Dunya*.
Until my heart turned around and said,

"This place is a dream, but I have dreams of my own."

What is hidden cannot stay hidden,
to the *Knower* of all things.

For my heart that is filled with what is written,
Oh Allah, do not attach my heart to the unwritten.

Listen to the words of the Qur'an.
Understand it deeply.
Let the meanings weave itself into the fabric of your heart.

This is the true reverence of our being.

mind&serenity

mindofserenity

THE ENCOUNTER

Chapter Two

The Encounter

We are all on a journey of searching.

But how do we know when to stop? It is the moment of realization that lost souls are longing for when they have found what they have been looking for.

The moment of the encounter. Steeping so deeply into what I was desperate to find and it was through Allah's mercy that opened my eyes. I had learned so much about myself, my faults, my weaknesses, my pride, and my selfishness. This moment of encountering my imperfections had broken me into pure vulnerability. Little did I know that this was the cure. A mercy. Being broken does not mean failure or downfall. Being broken is a sign of growth and transition; it is a door for you to reach your truest potential. It is a second chance to be better, a mercy given to undo what is weighing you down.

In my younger years, I had never truly acknowledged what Islam was. My upbringing was stern and ignorant of anything that differs from Catholicism. My home, my family, my school, and the years within, were filled with Christian influences. I was only 16 when I truly learned what Muslims are. This goes to show the ignorance of my mind that never circulated outside of its element. I remember being quite wordlessly surprised by the similarities between the religions (aside from the major differences of course). The ideas and values within Islam felt much more comprehensive when I, for an aeon, was never certain about the idea that God could be 3 things at once. *God,* to me, has always been singular. Hearing the biblical stories from a twisted and disoriented point of view during my childhood, it was evident that God was one god.

La ilaha illallah. I bought my first Qur'an in 2016 in secrecy. From that day onwards the next 4-5 years sparked my journey to Islam.

I remember being at my lowest state when everything around me was falling apart. My relationship with my family, and my friends at the time were all falling apart as I allow myself to drown in severe sadness. There were many things and reasons that I must keep to myself that led me to that state of despair. It was January 25th, 2020, after months of unhappiness I remember there was a switch that flipped so suddenly inside of me. My heart lived in the dark for so long that I had no hope that light will ever enter it again. But it did.

This was one of my very first encounters with inner peace. I had finally laid my pride to rest and surrendered to Allah at the start of my journey as a Muslim. Of course, I cannot ignore the worries ahead of me and what my family and friends would think of me. But at that very moment, I breathed in all my bitter memories, my tightened emotions, my pride and struggles that had led up to this, and breathed it away uttering the *Shahada*. It was this *Ayah* that kept ringing in my mind and learning what *Tawakkul* truly means:

(Allah [Alone] is sufficient for us, and He is the Best Disposer of affairs [for us].)
Qur'an 3: 173

Allah knows before the words have met our tongue, before the touches of our hands, before our tears meet the floor. Understanding that no matter what we lose in this life, there will be nothing compared to the depth of loss if we were to lose Allah in our lives. The *most sufficient*, Allah is the ultimate fulfiller of our needs, desires, and wishes. *The Best Disposer of affairs,* we have to understand what we desire and pray for, may not always be khayr for us. We must sincerely place our faith in Allah's disposal, what he takes away from our life and what he brings to it. When we find ourselves in a storm, it is difficult to remain level-headed and place our trust in Allah. There will be days of rain and darkness, but the sun always rises. Through this life, we must constantly, carry a good opinion of Allah and what is decreed for us. It is trusting and holding on to the faith that the light of Allah's protection will come. That his wisdom, his mercy, and love *will* greet us at the end of every tunnel.

I remember my father once asked me:

"*Are you safe? Are you Happy?*"

It was the moment that I knew as a father, that despite what he thought about Islam, the misconceptions, the misunderstandings, and miscommunications, all he wanted was to be assured that he did not fail his daughter by becoming Muslim. To show him that there was nothing to fear or to worry about. That leaving my old life is a gift, not something to grieve about. It was a gift of relief, knowing he trusted me and these changes, uncertain of what my future holds. It seems to be the same way as I have placed my trust in Allah, to carry a good opinion of what may come. I used to carry this thought that one day, this will become too much for those around me. That there will come a time that I would be left behind for the change I was making. I built up all this strength to prepare for that moment. But how can one ever prepare for a moment like that? Despite it all, he didn't walk away and gave me the chance to show him. It is one of the greatest gifts that Allah has given me for my patience.

Through loneliness, I was alone with my connection to Allah and my greatest grief was the stricken realization of my pride that kept me apart from *Him*.

mindofserenity

The person we should inspire to,
to learn and to know of,
is the person we are written to be.
When regret has become lessons,
emptiness has found meaning,
and all the deceit that was created
has turned into purity and truth.

Change is *a must, inevitability, a promise.*

I thought that I knew best. To believe that solitude was the place for me. For my sake, I thought to myself,

"Perhaps, this could make me better."

mindofserenity

We have the audacity to have pride as high as
the mountains.
Only to be buried beneath them.

mindofserenity

All I ever learned, in my time alone, was misery and despicable loneliness.

I thought that I knew best, to rob myself of moments; Moments of joy, moments of thankfulness. Moments had I wish to be shared with a loved one. When we are made to belong, to be companions and to be with one another. The purest of happiness is amongst our beloved ones.

But my pride took the best of me. My ignorance has stolen from me.

I thought I knew best, to live a life without humility.

You will find what you had lost.

It may not return as it was before, perhaps this is for the better. Perhaps it will return as something you needed, rather than what you desired. Only *Allah* knows the truth, only He knows what is best for you.

You cannot conquer the mountains,
without first climbing the troubles that conquer your heart.

Amongst the unknown,
is an undying flame that the usual eyes cannot see.

To recognize whose hearts are on fire,
and whose hearts are bind to dust.

Only when, the darkest shall depart from this world.
Only then, the brightest shall depart into its eternal home.

Every pain, every hardship, has been a hidden blessing.
Better yet,

Allah has kept it secret.

mindofserenity

Know that your heart does not belong here.
There is nothing from this world that could break it.

mindofserenity

Sometimes we need to acknowledge that pain,
is the pursuit of peace.

Because with complete surrender comes the inevitable, peace.
With the complete surrender of your pride,
there is humility.

If we want peace for this world,
we must first be the one to give it.

If you could teach Wisdom, it is the
greatest gift one could teach.
You are giving a glimpse of eternity.
Most importantly, *peace*.

Your imperfections may guide you.
Better than the pride that keeps you arrogant.
Just like wisdom gives you silence,
yet it is louder than ignorance.

If someone were to share wisdom with you
which you already have the knowledge of, do
not stop them. Let them believe they are
teaching you something new. You will see the
noor in their face, in their voice, in their eyes.
Do not rob that from them. There is no greater
feeling of gifting wisdom to others.
Let their words flow and you will see they even
surprise themselves sometimes.

It is a beautiful experience for you to witness,
and for them to feel.
Let them be.

You deserve the peace you bring to others.
The warmth that you cloak to the cold hearts.

You deserve the love and every tenderness.
The compassion you have shown. You deserve much more than the world could ever offer.

To heal and to love, is
to trust in *His* grace
alone.

mindofserenity

It was though my soul has searched for *You*.
Beyond its capacity for many years.

Our soul encompasses many things

be wary and generous with what you seek.
May it find well, and enrich it with the
knowledge of our *deen.*

Each breath must radiate of *khayr*

What serves as a nurturer, a comfort, a brace for others, is the beauty and elegance of our utterance.

With every touch must be gentle and graceful; that
pain cannot reach,
no harm to place us in peril.

We are not alone in this path.
We must seek and bestow help to each other.
We are, after all, born with tenderness from a
common divinity;

The Most Gracious, the Most Merciful

Preserve your purity and enrich it with
honour, knowledge, and beauty.
May it serve as a helping hand, and may it
give rise to fellow pursuers.

Purity is contagious

mindoßerenity

mindofserenity

THE FINDING

Chapter Three

The Finding

The Finding; also known as the reunion, the coming, *togetherness*.

The first few months of my reversion were incredibly lonesome. The days of my first Ramadan as a Muslim felt like an eternity after spending evenings of my *iftars* alone. I was fearful and anxious to reach out to the community, so I kept to myself. It was not long until I began yearning for companions. Since then, I have made beautiful and meaningful connections with many sisters across the world that has aided my connection in my *deen*. Also meeting with many reverts and sharing our experiences and struggles, enabled my healing and hope for the betterment of our future. It was difficult at times to hear some stories that had pained and darkened the experience of some. It is not my place to share their stories here, but if you could trust my word, after hearing what I have heard, I pray for you to have a little compassion, learn to avoid making false assumptions, and speak kindly. It breaks my heart knowing the pain many go through for simply believing in Allah and following his commands. Not every story of a revert or even a born Muslim, finding their way to Allah is beautiful and kind. But it is the most valuable and rewarding experience in our lifetime.

> *"But perhaps you hate a thing and it is good for you, and perhaps you love a thing and it is bad for you. And Allah Knows, while you know not."*
> *(Quran 2:216)*

We mourn for our soul that had finally lost all that is left inside. The pieces that we left behind that were once fighting for you to conquer. It is one of the most heartbreaking experiences that any human can go through is to watch yourself wither and fall into pieces, after standing for so long. Until we wonder what is left inside and for a moment, seemed forever lost. But we wait, and we wait. For the beauty of life that is yet to come. Only for life to once again break in front of you. Only for you, to watch it build and begin once again. Through the beautiful and dark moments, we accept that this is simply life. The finding, the acceptance is the most honourable moment and through that we finally find peace. We look back into our remaining pieces, as they slowly build the bridge that would never make us fall again. You hold on to that piece of faith, like a rope to pull you back into the light again.

We forget that not only can we reunite with our loved ones and companions, but in life, we can also reunite with ourselves and with Allah. The blessing of being divinely guided can lead our broken selves to be healed and bonded together, the distance between us and our lord has been mercifully shortened. This is the highest, most significant form of reunification. These experiences are all so casually bittersweet, cruel but most worthy and valuable to our soul.

Thinking about my past life feels wordlessly distant, completely different, and unrecognizable. *SubhanAllah,* I truly believe in the potential of change, that anyone can truly flip their life from one end of a spectrum to the other. Islam did not begin targeting the pious. They were once wrongdoers, sinners, people with darkened hearts and guilty hands. It is one of the many wonders of Islam, guiding those to the origins of their hearts.

mindofserenity

Until the voice of your heart is silent,
you are not broken.

mindofserenity

The only person that can take away your faith is yourself.
Even if the world is breaking at your feet,
it is your faith that carries you.

mindofserenity

So may our faith carry us high,
to the light of our *Creator*.

And if our legs stop working,
may our hearts keep going.

mindofserenity

When you realize your soul is made for the
beyond, follow it.
Our faith will carry us through, and we will rebuild
our broken pieces.

mindoserenity

And the heart will say,
"I am home"

There was nothing more
than I ever wanted than the
Akhirah.

mindofserenity

We yearn for a place we do not belong,
to remind our souls of our true home.

For the lover of the soul, and the lover of souls.
May you protect it from this world,
until it meets its true home.

mindofserenity

Eventually, our hearts will tire
from this world.
So when it wanders off,

let it run.

Oh *Allah,* even if the world pushes me to my knees,
I pray that my heart will never stop running
towards *You.*

Pray for what is beyond this *Dunya*, to attain what cannot be found.

Maybe that is why faith has stopped,
and the hearts are cold and veiled.

There is no recognition nor compassion
between the souls, if they are blinded by their own stale hearts.

Allah's mercy will *always* be greater than
all the riches of this world.

*Within time, the promised words of Allah
will come.*

Trust in *Allah*.
You will learn soon
enough.

Pray
because who knows when the storm will
come again.

When there is a battle within us, sometimes it is the only hope we have. To know a part of ourselves are still fighting, against what has already given up.

mindoserenity

Life will always begin again,
and it can always be found.
It does not come in one shape but many
forms.

Sometimes beautifully all at once

It is enough for me
to see how this world grows and start again,
even after death.

mindofserenity

mindofserenity

THE LESSONS

Chapter Four

The Lessons

To my younger self:

If only you knew what these lessons meant.

One of the key signs of knowing that you are high in pride is to live in a constant state of denial. Perhaps there are ways, painful ways that Allah will teach us. If we fail to learn it time and time again. When something or someone is not written in our decree, we become in denial of it. Allah will show us the bittersweet truth, the profound reason behind this. And this may be, a gradual, most heartbreaking experience; *the opening of one's heart.* The realization of truth, the grief, and the mourning of the time we have lost as we were living in the denial of truth and we grieve, not only for what we have accepted we have lost but for the knowledge that if we had learned of it sooner, perhaps life would have been better. When this moment comes, there will be an ache in the heart that may feel eternal but in truth, this is simply the opening and the beginning of one's heart to a gifted life that is incomparable to any thought of otherwise.

I have learned the true meaning of loss. My ultimate lesson; the loss of my loved ones, the loss of those who I had thought was good for me, and the loss of all the pleasures of life turned out to be my biggest enemy. I was stripped from myself and I had lost myself. Most importantly, I lost Allah. Until today, I do not have the strength to articulate my story in a way without breaking down. It has become a memory that I no longer claim from the person I am today, but the memory of a person I no longer am. Though the memory has numbed, my every attempt to recollect still pains me as if the wound has never healed.

Had I known this was a mercy that had saved me from myself. To learn I was no longer in the presence of the sin but the presence of the most divine. This is the process of purification to undo the once broken and hopeless self.

I remember the first time I prayed. I had prayed previously with my Muslim companions at the time but not with the intention of worship, but out of curiosity and interest. It was during my first Ramadan and I felt the pressure of the duty of *Salah*. But how can one offer it if they do not know how to? There was this guilt and fear I had felt that was very familiar with the fear that I had before reverting. I feared I would not be enough to live with the values of a Muslim, to follow the commands of Allah and the Sunnah of our Prophet *Sallallahu Alayhi Wa Sallam* (peace be upon him) with full surrender that my lifestyle would not allow it. But it was this fear that stole 4 years from becoming a Muslim. I began to understand and accept that this will be a gradual, learning experience. To be like a child learning how to pray for the first time, how to do *wudu*, and memorizing the ayahs. I knew that I would be expecting imperfection and mistakes as a new Muslim. But learning that the mercy of Allah is deeper than the ocean's depths and caves themselves is enough for me to overcome this fear and fulfil my spiritual duties for my new identity. I cannot explain the beautiful feeling when you have finally memorized the prayers; *Surah Al-Fatiha, Tashahhud,* and the gestures of *Qiyām, Ruku, and Sujood* without watching a video or looking at a piece of paper. *SubhanAllah...* I feared I would not be capable enough to pray independently and as the promise of Allah became evident that he will provide if you have good intentions, it will truly prevail. This lesson followed me through the rest of my journey toward the path to Allah.

The Messenger of Allah (ﷺ) said,

"If anyone constantly seeks pardon (from Allah), Allah will appoint for him a way out of every distress and a relief from every anxiety, and will provide sustenance for him from where he expects not."

[Abu Dawud].

The very first time wearing the *hijab* was incredibly liberating. It was the first time that my new identity has truly settled and I will be representing myself as a person of Islam, a community, a belief, and a collective faith. When I was Christian, there was no physical and conspicuous evidence in my appearance that communicated with those in public that this is my religion. Unless I was spotted at my local church or at my old catholic school. But even then, it cannot be certain. The first time I saw the *hijab*, the graceful modesty as a symbol of kind faith, I fell in love with what it meant. The 5 years of my life uncertain of the religion I belong to, was greatly frustrating as I did not have a secure place or belonging in both the Christian and Muslim communities. Wearing the *hijab* was my answer, my official identity shift, a promise I owed to myself. I had very little courage to wear it in front of my family as they never understood why I chose to wear it. They would argue with the fact that there are Muslim women out there who are practicing but are not covering their hair. So why did I choose to? "*Why did I choose to oppress myself?*" I knew better than to explain it in full depth that we all have our journey toward the *hijab*. It was a heartbreaking experience, to learn that if I were to attend to my social duties with my family in peace, is to not wear it when I am with them. But from this, I learned that there is a line between the obedience of Allah and the obedience to our parents. It is emphasized in the teachings to obey and have the utmost respect for our mothers and fathers. But to what extent? Should we still follow their orders even if it meant disobeying Allah's commands? But even with our loving parents, with our brothers and our sisters, our dear sons and daughters, grandparents, and companions;

Our love for them should not be greater than our love for Allah. Our fear of them should not be greater than our fear of Allah. That is the line we should not cross.

It was a change I am willing to commit to no matter how many times I may have fallen and failed to meet it, no matter how many criticisms I receive from my family, from those who once knew me, or the criticisms from Muslims themselves. Every hit of a hurtful tongue and hand will not tarnish and lessen my faith in Allah. Through this journey, I have lost the life I had once lived. With every moment of hurting, to healing, to finding the life I was destined to fulfil. These are the lessons I have found to keep. Lessons that had pained me. Lessons that had saved me.

Better yet lessons that Allah had blessed me in secret.

> *"Take one step towards me, and I will take ten steps towards you. Walk towards me, I will run towards you."*
>
> *Hadith Qudsi*

mindofserenity

Most of all
be kind to your own soul.

We fight against grief,
not knowing the peace it will bring.

mindofserenity

Oh, what a beautiful moment to witness the changes within someone.

Before you know it, they are divinely guided. The very last thing you expect to happen happens.
If you feel as though you may never change,

you more than capable than you think you are.

The storm won't last
forever. So when the sun
rises,
you will too.

Learn how to love the rain.
To embrace the hurricane. The hidden blessings are
within every drop, you do not learn the appreciation of
light without the clouds.
Like the trees when they are hit by the wind in every
storm, what do they do? They stand high.

They just keep growing.

When you become a companion of His light,
you will outlive every darkness that there is.

mindofserenity

You will have to realize the
blessing of *His* light
that conquers even the silence of
the dark.

Have tawakkul. Choose faith.
Sometimes all it takes is this
one step to be saved.

I wonder at times how life may have been better if I had
placed my trust in *Allah* sooner.

Perhaps, I would have been wiser, stronger, or more
deserving of those I treasure. If only, my pride hadn't been
too high as I was living in a state of denial.
"The truth always prevails," as they say. I knew then,
I should have listened and persevered.

mindofserenity

The beauty of Time;
when the truth comes with the sorrow,
the gift of resilience comes with it.

mindofserenity

How swift are our sorrows to leave, when we remember
the provider of our peace?

It is the hard truth if you want to survive
in this world.
To open your heart, you have to break it
and break it again.

There is so much strength in that.

mindofserenity

The softness in your heart is not a weakness.
It is *humility*.

Something that this world itself has failed
to attain.

mindoserenity

We do not always have to put on a brave face. We will face hardships and struggle because that is the way this *Dunya* is made. The only way we can get through it is to get *through* it. Accept it.

*You don't need to keep smiling,
you just need to keep going.*

So keep your heart satisfied.
Keep your faith burning in your heart even in the darkest moments.

True peace is not found within the quietest of
places or people.
It is beneath the noise, the chaos, the mess, and
the broken hearts.

It is acceptance.

You are the knowing, the dreaming, and the living in itself. You are not who you want to be, not who you were in the past.

The purest of you is who you are at this very moment.

mindoserenity

The most precious jewels live within the hidden.
Only to be found by those in the dark.
For they see the light,
within themselves first.

mind&serenity

The silence seems to grow when there is wisdom in the soul.

Learn to live soulfully.
To know one's soul, is to know *Allah*.

So follow the light of *Allah*.
Then watch yourself illuminate from within.

mindofserenity

And all the light will suffice,
for the one that drew the
veiling in their heart.

*Oh Allah, do not let me out of your light.
For I fear I may be drawn to this worldly life.*

Live in simplicity.
That is what life truly is.

Life is made so simple.
But we expect so much complexity,
we forget to honour every bit of it.

mind♄serenity

It is truly a skill to find comfort and peace,
underneath simplicity,
in the complexity of life.

True peace is not found within the
quietest of places and people. It is
beneath the noise, the chaos, the mess,
and the broken hearts.

It is *acceptance*.

Once you learn this, the state within you
remains undisturbed regardless of the
state outside of you.

mindofserenity

A soul so beautiful, the scent of their aura stays.
Whether they leave a room
or somebody's life.

mindofserenity

When a soul brings peace without its presence,
it has served its purpose.

Some hearts are like the sun. Even when it sets,
it illuminated with the stars.

Wherever the wind blows,
my faith in *Him* will follow.

mindoserenity

O Turner of Hearts,
may you turn our hearts towards *You*.

What more can I say except
Alhamdulillah

mindofserenity

mindofserenity

THE PROMISE

Chapter Five

The Promise

We often make promises to avoid uncertainties that may transgress into bigger problems in our lives, causing us sorrow. But this journey is different.

Some promises are made after we learn a lesson after going through a storm or a story to finally understand why things went wrong. I would not have learned Allah's promises if they were revealed to me at the beginning of my journey. You find them at your purest being, the rawest version of yourself, without your pride and your ego to blind you. I learned these promises at a time I was most broken. This was how the pain and the hurt bleed out and what enters is humility, the truth, the healing.

This is how the darkness comes out. This is how the light gets in.

In this life, we have promises fulfilled or awaiting their fulfilment. But the promises of Allah are the most deeply relieving in any given moment if one often remembers that Allah is the best provider, the All-Seeing, All-Hearing, and the *Responsive* one.

The promises may not always be clear. The one lesson I learned are to reflect well on His names, to read the words of the Qur'an, and listen deeply to the stories of the past prophets and the life of our greatest Prophet Muhammad *Sallallahu Alayhi Wa Sallam* (peace be upon him). Their trials and tribulations are unimaginable yet despite it all; they had relied on Allah's words and promises. This itself should give us hope and to never give up, particularly in times of despair. To see the way light travels to the highest horizon, to the deepest darkest of caves is evident of Allah's *Nūr* and Q*adr;* how deeply it travels to the darkest and broken hearts.

> **When I [finally] understood that my sustenance came from Allah, my heart was at peace.**
>
> *Hasan al-Basri al-Hilyah V.10,Pg.63*

I used to often dwell on the impacts and consequences of these changes, the impressions and views of who I am would change within my family, my culture, and my heritage. I did not know how much more heartbreak I could take from the judgments and abandonment I would face. Just as my family had been once before, I had once carried a bias and pessimistic presumption of Islam and those who follow the religion. I would have to take that extra step to prove them wrong and I was sceptical if I could do so alone.

But *Alhamdulillah.*

There will always be limitations when we pursue something in great depth and passion such as the fear and uncertainty of its potential to benefit us. But, with enough self-belief, our willingness, as human nature has it, will always defeat our incapability and our inward thoughts of ourselves. We are destined for strength, perseverance, and patience. We just need to believe it.

mindofserenity

Do not think that world will favour you and I.
For *Jannah* awaits to be called *home*.

When the possibility of the unknown has come, leaving unsaid words astray.
Only the good shall remain and all our blessings shall rise from the pain.

And no peace is ever lost if *Allah* is embedded in our hearts.

Even if the whole world does not see your
kindness,
it cannot compare to the reward
Allah will give you for it.

When the love of *Allah* reigns,
no darkness can hide the *noor* in
your eyes.

mindofserenity

Learn to live soulfully.
To know one's soul is to know Allah.

mindoserenity

The heart yearns for what it once was.
And I yearn for the light, even though it burns.
Because without it,
I will surely be in darkness.

Beware of those in the sea of sorrows;
they know what it takes to keep
themselves from drowning.

Strength is for the hearts of *noor*.
Which no darkness can overshadow,
no pain that can overbear.

If we open our eyes,
we shall see the light.
If we open our hearts,
we may *become it.*

mindofserenity

There is always wisdom in what is concealed.
Like a scar waiting to be healed.

If you knew that *Allah knows* what your
heart needed,
why do you grieve from what he has
taken from it?

So have patience.
Because patience is gratifying.
When one has mastered patience,
they have mastered the art of gratitude.

mindofserenity

You will meet yourself.
Over and over. At times you are broken, down to your
knees. At times you have never felt the most
alive, greater than the mountains you have conquered.

You will meet yourself and realize you were not alone.
But Allah has been there with you.

It is not the rain that troubles
you, but the fear of the storm.
Nor the highest of mountains,
but the depth of the fall. Not the
sea, the darkness, the silence.
But within you that you lack;

Tawakkul

No matter how much you fight. No matter how much life
may pain.
Only by the *remembrance* of *Allah*
can take it all away.

When you live in a state of remembrance,
the whole world becomes a garden.
Just wait for the rain to pass.

It is neither time nor a place that does the healing, rather *sabr* and *tawakkul* in *Him* is the cure for all bleeding.

You cannot fight your tears, you must let them fall.
Just as *Allah* has blessed the earth with rain,
a garden shall grow from it all.

mindoserenity

mindofserenity

Poetry

The Beginning

I have never told anyone how hard the beginning of this journey was for me. Perhaps, I wrote it and hinted at it in the most simplest and casual way I can. The truth is, becoming Muslim did not feel like a blessing at first. It was full of tests, failures, and disappointments. I unveiled my weaknesses, my faults that I soon learned this is what I needed to fix. Though I had not once doubted that this decision was the best thing, and the only thing I did right in my life. When you are being tested, you are faced with two responses; to be kind, to remember, to rely upon or to refuse, to silence any acknowledgement or trust in the higher being, to leave.

Endurance becomes an instinct.

Faith becomes second nature.

Patience, if you have it, is a gift that keeps giving and a promise unbroken.

This was the beginning of my ending.
 The start of a beautiful journey.
 A reset of a tragic story.

Jannah

Be free from the broken souls that strive for nothing but darkness
Be free from the daylight liars in the disguise of purity and truth
Be free from the burning desires that leave you in despair
Be free from the pursuits of pain in the mask of freedom

Be free of them and live *here* in peace

The Delicacy of Time

In all things that are timeless,
time remains to be the greatest distance

Time that have been lost or yet to be found.
Time of the unknown in the mask of uncertainty.
Time that is trapped waiting to be freed.
Constantly moving through moments
or stillness in seconds.

We are all missing, waiting, beginning.

Either searching for time, or for things to pass it.
Until there is no time at all. Until it is too late.
We had mistaken time and souls to be the same.

mindofserenity

Islam will always be the most simplest and extraordinary answer

No complications, no leeway or sugarcoated messages. Every answer we search for, undoubtedly comes before us, one way or another; Through the words of another, an ayah in the Qur'an, a page of a book, a spoken dua or the utter of remembrance.

The answers are there from the stars to our fingertips

The Entirety of Love

A love deeper than the depths of the sea.
A love that could awaken a soul that had lain for years.
A love that could bring this earth back to life and fill the thirsts of the quenched hearts.

A love with more than one definition or one way of
loving. But is seen through,
A mother's hand
A child's call
A bee and its sweet honey
The faith of the poor and the generosity of the rich
From the writer's hand to their reader's hearts
The helping hand of standing for the fallen

A love undefined, unconditional and distinct

Resilience

The truth of a resilient heart is not overcoming
the storm that eventually passes, but facing the
damage the storm has done. There is always
strength when you overcome the storms.
But to look at what it has broken, what is left
behind, and what is no longer there, is the real
test of resilience.

We have survived many storms together and it is
up to us if we choose to stay risen.

From everything that exists

there is a cause for every part of it.
The signs are there, from the stars to our fingerprints.
There is a code in all creations, evident of a *Creator*.
A unique pattern in every natural phenomenon,
there is wisdom in all things unexplainable.

Balance

To swim in the sea of sorrows
but to stay floating

To climb the mountains of calamities
but to keep climbing

Like the trees in every wind of a storm
but stay standing

With every loss we have faced
every grief we have endured
every blessing that was gifted

*Each time Allah has answered your prayers
you must keep praying*

Meet me in the sea of tranquility

It is that moment when we are floating and we stare right into the face of the sky. The noise of this world is unheard, drowning along with our broken thoughts and sorrows. That state of peace of just floating in the middle of a sea, a lake or a pool as you stare at that infinite sky.

When everything is blue around you, but you do not feel that blue *inside* you.

How can I live a life without you when you have become a part of me?

You are my eyes
for the things I cannot see

You are my lips
for the words I cannot speak

You are my hands
for the things I cannot reach

You are my lungs
for the days I cannot breathe

We tend to forget, even if it is just for a moment, that we do not hold control over what is decided for us

It is sometimes hard to differentiate, despite the obvious abstract, between our thoughts and feelings.
When we become overwhelmed with our over thinking we suddenly doubt what is in front of us.

We need to trust that in all of our works and all of our moments, *Allah* has willed it to be blessing, particularly at times it may not seem like it.

Rise

The stars do not leave even when the sun has risen

So when all pain has come forth
and your mountains have
crumbled before you
your darkness has overshadowed you
or the seas has overwhelmed you

Remember
Allah will not leave, even when you are falling

The war of acceptance

It is not how or what things appears to be
as it is their divine decree

But the war is when our hearts refuses to see

Silence

Silence can sometimes be brutal.
It can be heartbreak to a soul.
A yearning. A longing. An absence of life,
colour and feeling.
But what is most certain and deeply relieving,

Silence is never constant, always breaking.

Feign

In the life that I thought to be of feigned truth

Light was simply from candles
Peace only came from rain
Warmth resided from the sun
Hope to be followed with pain

Faith was only remains of ink on a page until I had
found it in my heart as I prayed.

Love

The heart falls in love all the time. Not in the way we think it does, but if you pay attention…

We fall in love when we feel the warmth of the sun on our faces. When we see the stars. When we read a quote and it touches our hearts. When we see the unity of humanity in a very cruel world. Or when we accept pain as a blessing for our souls.

Our hearts balances our bodies; it closes and opens, it breaks and becomes whole again. Just like life. It moves and imitates life within the darkest and beautiful moments, the calm and the chaos.

When you realize this, the peace within you is incomparable and continuous.

Reflections

There are these moments that your soul just tells you to stop.
To pause your words, your phone,
your book, and your thoughts.
Begging you to reflect on the wonders and life within you,
before this world drowns you with it.
You look at the clouds, the sea,
and the trees and you feel stillness.
Though they are in constant motion.

So become what you observe and seek,
you are already what you wish to be.

Our unheard voices

Silence at times,
coalesce of our hidden emotions and thoughts
waiting to be expelled.
It is a strange phenomenon,
to be utterly overwhelmed with deep quietness.

The Journey

Islam is a gift that touches and moves the hearts of those open to it. Some are moved slowly, while others may be an instant change. If you wish to have *sabr* upon yourself, have *sabr* for others as well. Allah has already written each moment of our time, so aid them beautifully in their journey to Islam.

Do not let your actions and words become someone's obstacle to be amongst the blessed ones.

Unity

The oneness of the *ummah* should be like the birds
of a flock.

Take heed of the birds as they fly harmoniously in
unity. That no distance between them can keep
each other from flying in one path;
all guided to where their fate lies.
In unity, no matter the speed or distance,
they move together as one.

Protect your soul, your heart,
your whole

Protect your soul.
This *dunya* is not your home.
Conquer your desires; do not fall for the
feigned desires. In the eyes of envy, this
world will delude you to a blissful ending.
But in the eyes of the wise, the knowing of
our true home is an eternal blessing.

So protect your soul
your heart
your whole

Faith is like a river

Sometimes gushing all at once. Sometimes flowing gently,
quietly, and calm.
Endless and continuous, it strengthens the life around it.
Let faith be a continuous flow inside of you,
expect the tides and the stillness.
Let it soften the hearts of stone,
and let it be *constant*.

The pursuit of knowledge is the pursuit of inner peace

but this world will trick you into thinking
that ignorance is bliss

You will find those stuck in their thoughts, with sorrows and worries growing without an end.
They will never climb the mountains they see, or be the rising of the sun they only wish to be.
They reside to what they know, only to be lost into the unknown. But in the path of knowledge, the heart grows with clarity.
Clarity for all things from the desert to the seas.

Life becomes light, wherever they are and whatever they see.

Chosen

There are souls that reside in this life
like stars in the night sky

Hearts that had raised with the sun
no stranger of arising from the dark

Reminders of the fallen who climbed
guided by their own light

Chosen by our most *Beloved*
He had led the blessed to become one

***How can my greatest love,
not be Allah?***

The love of *Allah*

The only love that will return

In the midst of the broken hearts

In the midst of what seems to be eternal uncertainty

In the midst within the sorrowful souls

In the deepest depth of despair

It is the only love that will return

***Many of those with a sorrowful beginning
will find themselves in a blissful ending***

It is great wisdom to reflect on the life you once lived. And in the wonder, you found the life you were destined to fulfill.

You may regret the life you once lived, the moments and stories you may never speak of aloud. But in truth, it has led you to the path you were destined to walk on. You might not have realised it then, or have yet to realise it now.

But if you have trust in *Him*,
you are already on that path to healing.

***Do not think that you are alone,
for Allah has a written a name
for each of us all***

Allah created the trees in grand numbers
the sun with the spectrum of light
the birds of a dozen flocks
the mountains with neighbouring heights

And man to live together as one

***The pursuit of the wise has no measure
only that wisdom often comes hand in hand with
mystery***

Gaining new knowledge is like climbing to the top of the mountain and having the whole world beneath you. But looking up, having another world yet to discover.

There will always be other mountains to climb, rivers to swim by, and skies to fly. Once you start, the only choice you have is to keep going.

The journey only ends when *you* do.

It is no secret that gentleness is contagious

As it bridges the hearts,
provokes the peace between lovers and strangers.

Like a mother to her dear child,
gentleness becomes their impenetrable strength and tender bond

Gentleness towards the self, when there is no other
that shares your pulse
is freedom from your dark thoughts.

Become graceful with your words and silence

As elegance becomes your language

Despite of your despairs,
your heart remains irenic

Captivated by the essence
of your soul's fragrance

*Perhaps thing do not fall apart
but fall into place*

I suppose it had never occurred to me nor had I ever understood why things must fall apart before they can mend themselves.
Perhaps it is just how we look at it;

Perhaps things do not fall apart but fall into place.

We often refuse to accept what it has become because we already settled for what it used to be.
We fight against change, against unfamiliarity.
Why do we fight when we are given what is rightfully better?

And the real tragedy within is accepting less than what we deserve when we are owed greater than infinity.

mindofserenity

***If I hadn't found you in this life,
I will find you in my dreams.***

I will look for you in the stars
I will seek for you through the beautiful words of
a poet, in its eternal language
I hadn't found you in *this life*
I hope to find you in the *next*

Our stories may be written by the same writer, though we were not written for each other.

It is a strange thing, dealing with loss when death played no part. As with all journeys, we are expected to continue. But who we have begun with is no longer with us.

How do we deal with loss between us, when you and I are in the same room?

Sometimes the people we grow up with, those we have met in the beginning are not written for what is to come for the rest of our lives. Sometimes holding on holds a greater burden than finally letting go. Lessons come and go as experiences or people.

As lessons reach their inevitable end, eventually, we also have to move on.

Learn to forgive yourself

Your past and distant self, every mistake and misstep.
This world teaches us that our errors are unforgivable. It is only an error if you have not learned from it. Every lesson is a step toward growth and healing. But a lesson cannot appear out of anything. It stems from our faults and without our faults we have nothing to learn and gain in life.
We have nothing to prove to Allah.

You have learned to be better, to be wiser and prudent.
You at least owe that to yourself.

The past seems so far away until something places you back to that very moment

Passing by a familiar scent,
picking up an old childhood book
flipping through old photographs and written letters
the sound of the sea and wind that you grew up listening to.

Seeing an old face you once looked up
to now they are looking up to you.

It is wondering when and why things went wrong,
and learning how it became right.

It is cruelly bittersweet thinking where the years have gone
until I find myself in moments as if I have never left.

The desert asked,

"Oh Sun, why have you stayed?
When all things of life have left me?
I am nothing but a cloudless being, even a single drop of
rain will not reach me.
I am empty."

The sun replied,

"You were once a great sea.
Surrounded by the pleasures of life, this became your
biggest enemy.
Our Lord has stripped you from yourself.
Now, only you can illuminate the stars that no man has
seen. Your grains hold wisdom for the hopeless souls.

You are not the absence of life,
but in the presence of Allah."

Anger

It is not always the flames that fuels our
anger,
but the depth whilst drowning in our sorrows.
It is not always the hardening of the heart,
but its fragile glass.
Anger is not always fire or violence,
but a fatal stillness;
a numbness, an absence,

a consequence of a heart in excessive silence.

***The beauty of our garments, that we call
Faith***

The strength of our modesty and persistence,
despite misconstrue.
To be amongst those whom Allah loves,
shall find ease in what they endure.

The most beloved heart is filled with flaws.

Arrogance and ignorance are the poison for purity. Humility is accepting our vulnerabilities, lowering our pride and gaining wisdom to persist self-improvement.
Striving for change, striving for refinement.

*Allah loves those who strive for him
and him only.*

***We must understand that everything comes,
and everything leaves in its due time***

Even a fruit before it is harvested
A leaf falling from a tree
The rising of the sun in the early dawn
The setting of the sun before the coming of twilight

It is dangerous to rush things if they come or leave before its given time.
We might miss the endless possibilities of a fruit, if it is not ready to be reaped.

Understand the *rizq* of Allah

Because it will leave sooner as it came,
and regret will reach you before gratitude can relieve you.

**There is nothing but the bitter silence
that echoes through these walls**

Only but the pounding of a broken heart calling
for its Lord

Sabr without a word spoken

Tawakkul before life unfolds

Shukr amidst the calamities

These are the jewels of a believing heart
when one calls from distress Allah *surely*
responds

As travelers, as you leave the sun to meet the stars,
only then you will understand the beauty of endings.

And there is no loneliness for the traveler
if the path is just one path,
and all the hearts *Allah* moves become one.

mindofserenity

As I watch the sun rise,
I feel my soul rises too.

Until the stars arrive,
my heart awaits for *You*.

My heart will soon be
home.

mindofserenity

Calm your mind, strengthen your heart.
Lead a quiet, righteous life.

mindofserenity

I do not write from what I read,
but I write from what I have lived through. With
that, it is either a beautiful mystery or a dark
tragedy.

There is only one thing that is certain:
No one will ever truly know.

FURTHER NOTES AND ACKNOWLEDGEMENTS

The journey of continuously refining my passion for writing and sharing my most heartfelt, vulnerable, and sometimes painful, experiences as a *Revert*, through short and inconspicuous excerpts, had led me to a greater peace I cannot even imagine. I had conquered mountains I never thought I will ever climb through the mountains of great depth that showed me perseverance is key. Pouring my heart into this book and finally sharing my intimate experiences with those who had stayed since the very beginning, those I have met along the way, and those I have yet to meet who may have stumbled upon this work. For those who have shared their wonderful support, particularly through my darkest times. My family, though I had kept this secret hobby of mine, had grown to love and supported me despite life's changes, for those who remained with me and listened. For those who had left to teach me the true value and importance of meaningful companionship. My gratitude is to *you*. To whom my heart eternally belongs to and to whom I am eternally grateful for.

Most of all and above all, to **Allah**. To whom my gratitude is *never* enough.

I have stories I may never speak of aloud that my vulnerability may not be perfectly understood if they remained simply in a form of posts. Writing this book, allowed me to breathe what I once promised to remain concealed. But for my benefit, and the blessed position that Allah has allowed me to do, my heart goes to *you* for any goodness you may have found here. I am not alone in this journey, and that is my most comforting promise. As I have once said and promised to remember, to reflect in every work, in every effort, in everything that we strive for in this life:

"Be the kind of soul that others wish they could meet you a thousand times."

To be the best of who you are, your heart and your soul, for everyone that crosses your path.
Be simplistic and powerful with your words, be meaningful in your actions, and have purity in every intention that you make. With Allah in my heart, I want to make sure others see that first before they meet with me and that in itself is empowering in the most humble way.

I don't want to leave a mark in this world.
Allah already has.

Mindofserenity

mindofserenity

GLOSSARY

Allāh: Common name for God in the Arabic language

Ākhirah: Arabic term for **"the Hereafter"**

Alhamdulillah: Arabic phrase meaning "**praise be to God**", sometimes translated as "thank God"

Āyah: A verse in the Qur'an

Dunyā: refers to the temporal world and its earthly concerns and possessions, as opposed to the hereafter ('ākhirah)

Hijab: refers to head coverings worn by Muslim women

Iftar: the evening meal with which Muslims end their daily Ramadan fast at sunset.

Jannah: Muslim concept of heaven or paradise

La ilaha illallah: meaning "There is no God but God"

Nūr: (also known as noor) meaning **"light"**, **"The Divine Light"**

Qadr: meaning **"fate"**, **"divine fore-ordainment"**, **"predestination,"** but literally **"power"**

Qiyām: an integral part of the Islamic *salah*

Rizq: means whatever is of beneficial use and it also mean bestowal of something by Allah

Rukū: The act of belt-low bowing in standardized prayers, where the backbone should be in rest, before straightening up to go for *sujud*

Sabr: Islamic virtue of **"patience"** or **"endurance"**

Sajdah: **Sujūd**, the act of low bowing or prostration to God facing the qiblah

Salah: (Salat) ritual prayer that is obligatory for Muslims to perform five times a day

Sallallahu Alayhi Wa Sallam: meaning **"Peace be upon him"** A blessing commonly used by Muslims after mentioning the names of Prophet Muhammad (pbuh)

Shahada: the declaration of faith in one God (Allah) and His messenger

Shukr: meaning **"gratitude"** or **"thankfulness"**

SubhanAllah: '(all) praise be to God'. Used as a general expression of praise, gratitude, or relief

Sunnah: also spelled Sunna, are the traditions and practices of Prophet Muhammad (pbuh)

Tawakkul: to depend sincerely in one's heart upon Allah, reliance in Allah's plan

Tashahhud: also known as at-Tahiyyat, means **'greeting'** or **'salutation'**. It is recited when a person sits or kneels down during second rakah or last rakah of the prayer (*salah*)

Ummah: meaning "**community**" of Islam

Wuḍū: Islamic procedure for cleansing parts of the body, a type of ritual purification, or ablution

mindofserenity

Printed in Great Britain
by Amazon